BLAZERS

WEAPONS OF WAR

WEAPONS OF
WORLD WAR I

by Matt Doeden

Reading Consultant:
Barbara J. Fox
Reading Specialist
North Carolina State University

Content Consultant:
John C. Hendrickson
Adjunct Professor of History
Minnesota State University, Mankato

Capstone

Mankato, Minnesota

Blazers is published by Capstone Press,
151 Good Counsel Drive, P.O. Box 669, Mankato, Minnesota 56002.
www.capstonepress.com

Library of Congress Cataloging-in-Publication Data
Doeden, Matt.
    Weapons of World War I / by Matt Doeden.
    p. cm. — (Blazers. Weapons of war)
    Includes bibliographical references and index.
    Summary: "Describes the weapons used in battles during World War I,
including infantry weapons and heavy artillery such as howitzers and machine
guns" — Provided by publisher.
    ISBN-13: 978-1-4296-1971-4 (hardcover)
    ISBN-10: 1-4296-1971-6 (hardcover)
    1. Military weapons — History — 20th century — Juvenile literature.
2. World War, 1914–1918 — Equipment and supplies — Juvenile literature.
I. Title. II. Title: Weapons of World War One. III. Title: Weapons of World War 1.
IV. Series.
UJ815.D64 2009
523.409'041 — dc22   2008001990

Editorial Credits
Carrie A. Braulick, editor; Alison Thiele, set designer;
    Kyle Grenz, production designer; Jo Miller, photo researcher

Photo Credits
Alamy/ClassicStock, 9; Alamy/Mary Evans Picture Library, 13 (grenade
launcher); Alamy/Pictorial Press Ltd, 27 (top), 29 (submarine); Alamy/The
Print Collector, 5, 16; AP Images, 29 (armored car); Art Resource, N.Y./Erich
Lessing, 6; BigStockPhoto.com/sidonphotography, 21 (cannon); BigStockPhoto.
com/stacyb, 29 (biplane); Corbis, 15; Corbis/Bettmann, 24 (top); Corel, cover
(top), 10, 13 (Luger pistol); Dreamstime/Bellanordi, cover (bottom left), 13
(hand grenade); Getty Images Inc./Hulton Archive, 11 (top), 12; Getty Images
Inc./Hulton Archive/Imagno, 28; Getty Images Inc./Time Life Pictures/Mansell,
24 (bottom); The Granger Collection, New York, 25; The Granger Collection,
New York/ullstien bild, 18, 21 (Big Bertha howitzer); The Image Works/Alinari
Archives, 20 (bombs and missiles); The Image Works/Scherl/SV-Bilderdienst/
Lessman, 17, 20 (anti-aircraft missile); The Image Works/SSPL, 13 (rifle);
The Image Works/Topham, 29 (zeppelin); iStockphoto/Duncan Walker, 26;
iStockphoto/John Cairns, 21 (machine gun); iStockphoto/Sadikgulec, 27
(bottom); James P. Rowan, 21 (mortar), 29 (tank and battleship); © 2008
Jupiterimages Corporation, 13 (bayonet); NARA, 23; Shutterstock/Copestello, 21
(Prussian howitzer); Shutterstock/Marilyn Volan (grunge background elements),
all; Shutterstock/Zsolt Horvath, cover (bottom right), 13 (gas mask); www.
historicalimagebank.com, 11 (bottom), 13 (trench knife), 20 (shell)

TABLE OF CONTENTS

CHAPTER 1
Battle in the Trenches 4

CHAPTER 2
Infantry Weapons 8

CHAPTER 3
Battlefield Blasts 14

CHAPTER 4
From Land to Sea and Sky 22

Glossary 30
Read More 31
Internet Sites 31
Index 32

BATTLE IN THE TRENCHES

The clatter of gunfire fills
the air on a World War I (WWI)
battlefield. Soldiers duck down
in trenches. They all hope to
live through the day.

trench — a long, deep area cut into the
ground with dirt piled up on one side; WWI
armies dug trenches for a place to take cover.

WEAPON FACT

World War I was also called "The Great War" and "The War to End all Wars."

World War I raged from 1914 to 1918. Poisonous gas and airplanes were new weapons. Guns and `explosives` were used in earlier wars. But old or new, one thing was sure — WWI weapons were deadly.

`explosive` — a weapon designed to blow up after reaching its target

WEAPON FACT

France, Great Britain, Russia, and the United States were key players in WWI. These Allied nations fought the Central powers, which included Germany, Austria-Hungary, and Turkey.

INFANTRY WEAPONS

A WWI infantry soldier was never without his rifle. Soldiers used these guns to hit distant targets. U.S. soldiers pitted their Springfield M1903 rifles against the Germans' Mauser rifles.

infantry — the part of an army that fights on foot

rifle — a powerful gun with a long barrel that is fired from the shoulder

WEAPON FACT

Many rifles had long blades
called bayonets on their barrels.

Soldiers used other guns to shoot at closer targets. Pistols like the German Luger and the U.S. M1911 were easy to handle. Some U.S. soldiers used shotguns. These guns sprayed enemies with pellets.

German Luger pistol

Weapon Fact

Armies used poisonous gas for the first time in WWI. Soldiers wore gas masks to protect themselves.

Winchester model 1897 shotgun

German flamethrowers struck fear into soldiers everywhere. These long tubes spouted burning fuel. Hand grenades were another threat. Soldiers tossed or fired these small explosives into enemy trenches.

WEAPON FACT

Flamethrowers shot fire almost 50 feet (15 meters).

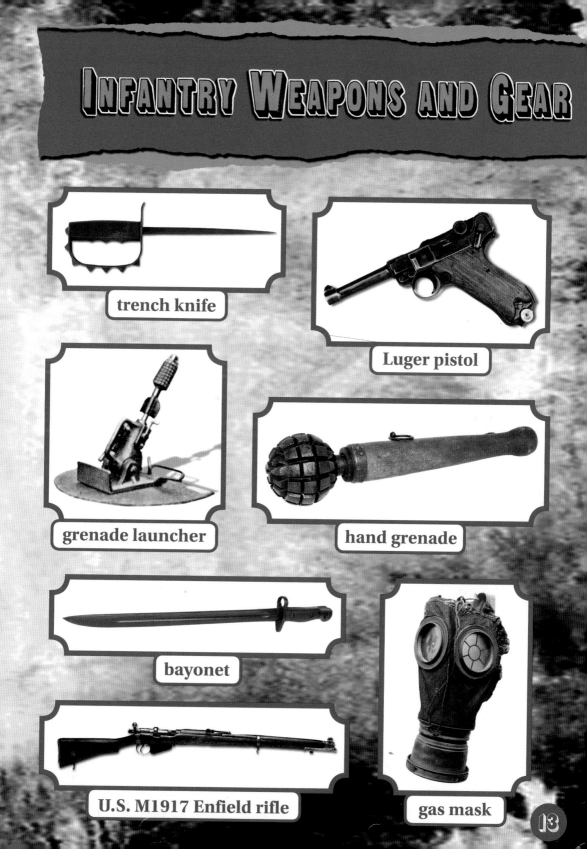

INFANTRY WEAPONS AND GEAR

trench knife

Luger pistol

grenade launcher

hand grenade

bayonet

U.S. M1917 Enfield rifle

gas mask

Battlefield Blasts

Trenches were filthy. But staying put kept soldiers safe from machine gun fire. These large guns shot hundreds of bullets each minute.

15

heavy Austrian mortar

The rumble of explosives was constant. Cannons called mortars rained shells onto soldiers. Anti-aircraft guns blasted missiles at enemy airplanes.

cannon — a large, heavy gun usually mounted on wheels or another supporting structure

missile — an explosive weapon thrown or launched at a distant target

anti-aircraft gun
loaded with missile

Big Bertha

When it came to cannons, howitzers were king. The German Big Bertha shot shells more than 7 miles (11 kilometers). Some of its shells weighed more than 250 pounds (113 kilograms)!

howitzer — a large cannon with a long barrel; howitzers fire shells high into the air and at distances of several miles.

HEAVY WEAPONS AND EXPLOSIVES

bombs and missiles (Austrian)

37-millimeter shell (French)

anti-aircraft missile

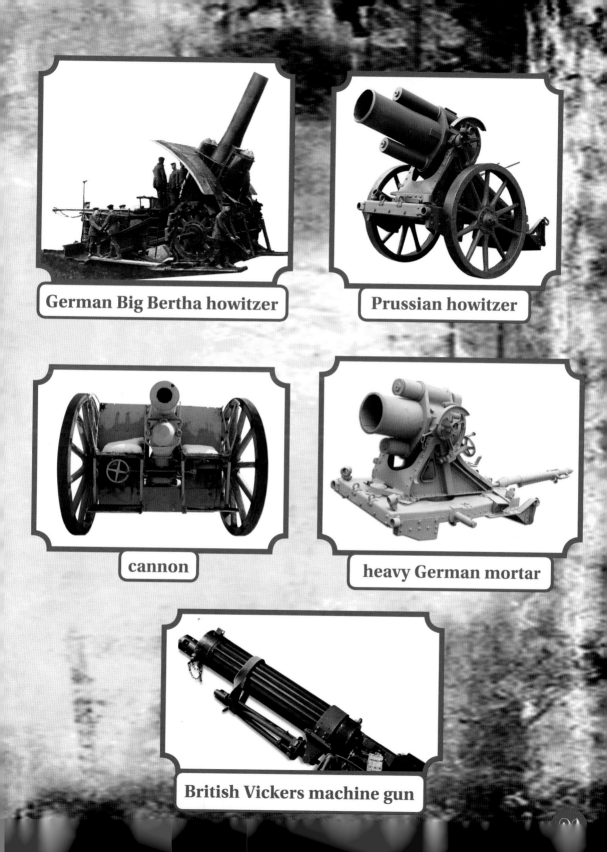

German Big Bertha howitzer

Prussian howitzer

cannon

heavy German mortar

British Vickers machine gun

From Land to Sea and Sky

Tanks were a new weapon. These armored vehicles on tracks often broke down. At first, they did little damage. But their big guns helped armies push through enemy lines later in the war.

armored — having a protective covering; WWI tanks had metal armor.

WEAPON FACT

Early tanks were also called landships.

WWI pilots dropping bombs

barrage balloon

WEAPON FACT

German barrage balloons looked similar to zeppelins. They kept enemy airplanes away from important places.

Other weapons traveled through the air. Airplane pilots shot each other down and dropped bombs. The Germans dropped bombs from airships called zeppelins.

British battleship

Warships blasted each other with gunfire. Submarines hid silently underwater. They shot torpedoes at enemy supply ships.

WEAPON FACT

Submarine crews watched out for sea mines.
Bumping one caused a deadly explosion.

WEAPON FACT

More than 8 million soldiers died during WWI. About 700,000 were American soldiers.

From rifles to airplanes, World War I was filled with deadly weapons. In 1918, the war ended. But updated models of its weapons proved their power in later wars.

VEHICLES

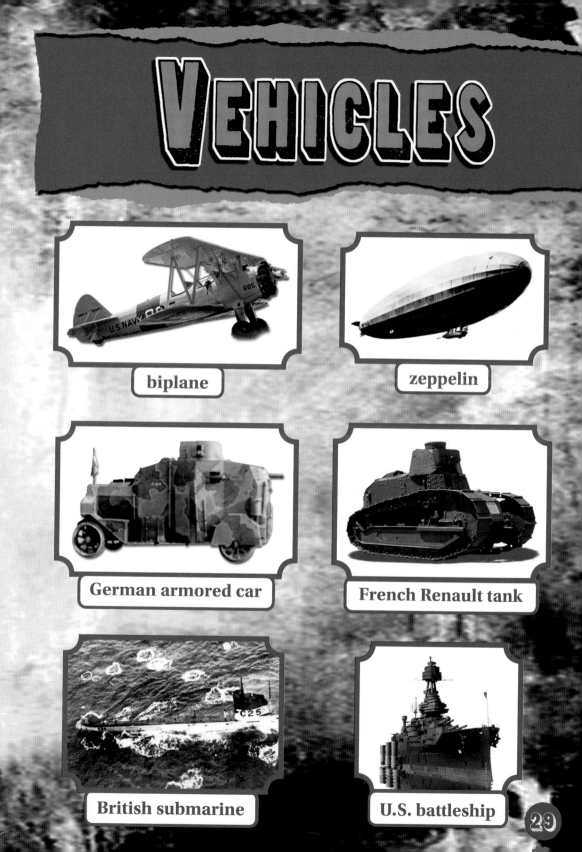

biplane

zeppelin

German armored car

French Renault tank

British submarine

U.S. battleship

GLOSSARY

armored (AR-muhrd) — having a protective covering; WWI tanks had metal armor.

barrel (BAYR-uhl) — the long, tube-shaped metal part of a gun through which bullets travel

cannon (KAN-uhn) — a large, heavy gun that usually has wheels and fires explosives

explosive (ik-SPLOH-siv) — a weapon designed to blow up after reaching its target

filthy (FILTH-ee) — very dirty

howitzer (HOU-uht-sur) — a long-barreled cannon that fires shells high into the air

infantry (IN-fuhn-tree) — the part of an army that fights on foot

missile (MISS-uhl) — an explosive weapon that is thrown or shot at a distant target

rifle (RYE-fuhl) — a long-barreled gun that is fired from the shoulder

torpedo (tor-PEE-doh) — an explosive missile that travels underwater

trench (TRENCH) — a long, deep area cut into the ground with dirt piled up on one side

READ MORE

Hamilton, John. *Weapons of World War I.* World War I. Edina, Minn.: Abdo, 2004.

Hibbert, Adam. *In the Trenches in World War I.* On the Front Line. Chicago: Raintree, 2006.

Parks, Peggy J. *Weapons.* Yesterday and Today. San Diego: Blackbirch Press, 2005.

INTERNET SITES

FactHound offers a safe, fun way to find Internet sites related to this book. All of the sites on FactHound have been researched by our staff.

Here's how:
1. Visit *www.facthound.com*
2. Choose your grade level.
3. Type in this book ID **1429619716** for age-appropriate sites. You may also browse subjects by clicking on letters, or by clicking on pictures and words.
4. Click on the **Fetch It** button.

FactHound will fetch the best sites for you!

INDEX

airplanes, 7, 16, 25, 28
airships. *See* zeppelins
Allied nations, 7
anti-aircraft guns, 16

barrage balloons, 25
bayonets, 9
bombs, 25
bullets, 14

cannons, 16, 19
    howitzers, 19
    mortars, 16
Central powers, 7

explosives, 7, 12, 16, 27

flamethrowers, 12

gas masks, 11

hand grenades, 12

infantry, 8

machine guns, 14
missiles, 16

pistols, 10
    Lugers, 10
    M1911s, 10
poisonous gas, 7, 11

rifles, 8, 9, 28
    Mausers, 8
    Springfield M1903s, 8

sea mines, 27
shells, 16, 19
shotguns, 10

tanks, 22, 23
torpedoes, 26
trenches, 4, 12, 14

warships, 26
    submarines, 26
    supply ships, 26

zeppelins, 25